# HOW TO SEE CONSCIOUSNESS

Cover photography: Dr. Anthony Kane (2023), *Untitled*.

*Anthony, from Australia, is an accomplished nature and wildlife photographer and, most of all, a great guy whom I had the pleasure of meeting during a trip to the Arctic. Anthony's photo captures the extraordinary encounter between a photographer (not Anthony) and a curious polar fox. During the encounter, the photographer in the picture didn't look up from his camera and missed the magical meeting with the frolicking fox—because he was looking for wildlife. Inadvertently, he showcased the perfect metaphor for not "seeing" consciousness.*

Marcel Eschauzier

# HOW TO SEE CONSCIOUSNESS

Rational Philosophy of Mind

BRUSSELS
XRLMEDIA
2023

Copyright © 2023 Marcel Eschauzier
All rights reserved. No part of this book may be reproduced or used in any matter without the written permission of the copyright owner except for the use of quotations in a book review.
ASIN B0CM9L2JP7 (ebook)
ISBN 979-8864675823 (paperback)

"The present is the only thing that has no end."

—Erwin Schrödinger

"Your knowledge is nothing but cowardice. No, really, that's all it is. You just want to put a little wall around infinity. And you're afraid to look on the other side of that wall. It's the truth."

—R-13 to D-503 in *We*, by Yevgeny Zamyatin

"The reason why our sentient, percipient and thinking ego is met nowhere within our scientific world picture can easily be indicated in seven words: because it is itself that world picture. It is identical with the whole and therefore cannot be contained in it as a part of it."

—Erwin Schrödinger

"There is obviously only one alternative, namely the unification of minds or consciousnesses. Their multiplicity is only apparent, in truth there is only one mind."

—Erwin Schrödinger

# CONTENTS

Introduction

    Abstract    1

    Background    3

    Objective    5

    Exposition    6

1 Scope and method    7

2 Irrational Western consciousness theories    10

3 The limitations of analytic philosophy    13

4 The non-existence of what memories refer to    17

5 The virtuous nondualism and reason circle—and its limitations    20

6 The inconceivable nature of consciousness    23

7 Nondualistic epistemology    25

8 Discussion    29

Conclusion 32

Acknowledgment 33

# INTRODUCTION

This short book presents the extended version of an academic philosophy-of-mind essay submitted September 28, 2023, for the CFP essay prize "Is Consciousness Fundamental?" This prize is part of the John-Templeton-Foundation-funded project "Panpsychism and Pan(en)theism: Philosophy of Mind Meets Philosophy of Religion," led by Philip Goff (Durham University) and Andrei A. Buckareff (Marist College). Added material includes an epistemology subchapter and quantum mechanics considerations.

The essay contains unexplained terms because it is written for specialist readers. Please note that the nondualistic paradigm differs from the conventional analytic and requires somewhat broader philosophy-of-mind interpretations. As an introduction, here is a short clarification:

- ✓ Dualism is consciousness theory explicitly or implicitly predicated on the human ability to know something other than consciousness. This differs from the traditional analytic understanding, which usually merely considers mind-body dualism.
- ✓ Monism is consciousness theory that defines the mind and the rest of the world as a single substance: pure mentality, pure physicality, or a third substance.

# INTRODUCTION

- ✓ Nondualism is consciousness theory that holds that the world can only be known as consciousness. It differs from monism in that consciousness is not definable as either mentality, physicality, or a third substance. Instead, it is the intrinsically undefinable concurrence of subject and object. Even so, all conscious human beings have an unobstructed view of consciousness and may readily see for themselves what it is. The only challenge is to know where to look.

# ABSTRACT

Dualistic consciousness theories are not rational because they require supernatural conjecture to account for the interaction problem. Analytic philosophy's consciousness theories, including all monisms such as panpsychism, suffer from explicit or implicit dualism.

Hume's challenge to reason in 1748 allowed analytic philosophy to gain prominence since the turn of the 20th century because it discredited inductive reason. Nondualism answers Hume's challenge to reason because it entails that subjectivity is the unique truth touchstone instead of an illusory mind-independent entity. Thus, nondualism justifies applying top-down inductive reason to study consciousness in contrast to the exclusively conceptual, bottom-up analytic approach. Reason based on nondual awareness approaches the subject-object concurrence from a position before its conceptualization into parts.

Thus, the rules of rational thought allow inducing the limits of what we can know about consciousness and reaching comprehensive ontological conclusions about consciousness in relation to the rest of the world. Notably, it must be concluded that consciousness is an inherently inconceivable substance that lacks a knowable efficient cause. This substance is ontologically identical to change and to the present. The

# ABSTRACT

universe can only be known to exist as consciousness because consciousness has no access to reality—a word that indicates something real beyond consciousness.

# BACKGROUND

This essay is written for the essay prize "Is Consciousness Fundamental?" on the question of whether consciousness is a fundamental feature of the universe, as part of the John-Templeton-Foundation-funded project, "Panpsychism and Pan(en)theism: Philosophy of Mind Meets Philosophy of Religion," led by Philip Goff (Durham University) and Andrei A. Buckareff (Marist College).

The author has a Master of Science in Industrial Engineering and Management Science from the Eindhoven University of Technology in the Netherlands and has lived and worked as an engineer and business consultant in various Western, Asian, and Latin American cultures. He is interested in Western and Eastern philosophy. In 2016, he had an insight that dispelled the illusion of duality, leading him to explore and contemplate the world's nondualistic nature. He has investigated why nondualism can be understood rationally but not conceptually, arguing for the primacy of the first-person perspective in metaphysics. He has published various books that aim at demystifying nondualism.

The crucial difference between monism and dualism versus nondualism is that the latter recognizes the primacy of unconceived knowledge. Hence, nondualism can only be entirely understood pre-conceptually, from a first-person perspective. It follows that the consciousness issue can be clarified but not entirely satisfactorily resolved by a mere text because texts are necessarily conceptual. This circumstance contributes to the ever-recurring confusion about consciousness, even though the consciousness issue has already been resolved by many, including over two-and-a-half thousand years ago by Lao Tzu in the Tao Te Ching.

# OBJECTIVE

The purpose of this essay is to reinstate inductive reason as the principal method of philosophical inquiry into consciousness. It argues that the centuries-old principles of rational thought, whose credibility suffered from the challenge to reason by Hume's Enquiry (1748), are a legitimate means to induce rational knowledge concerning consciousness and the world.

The principles of rational thought are predicated on ubiquitous empirical facts, sustain nondualism, and allow meaningful conclusions about consciousness. The dualistic paradigm provides less clarity than the nondualistic because the former involves the interaction problem. Thus, implicitly and explicitly dualistic consciousness theories, which are shown to include all monisms, confuse rather than clarify and should be rejected as not rational. It is argued that panpsychism is an example of such an implicitly dualistic monism.

# EXPOSITION

# 1

# SCOPE AND METHOD

This essay approaches the issue of consciousness via the human conscious mind. However, its conclusions are potentially also valid for subjects from the animal kingdom, extraterrestrial worlds, and artificial realms that share our human home universe.

The human conscious mind contains two types of content: content with a meaning that depends on present immediacy and content with a meaning that does not depend on present immediacy, hereafter referred to as immediate and mediated mind content. Consciousness has, by definition, a first-person perspective, so the meaning of mediated mind content must be auto-mediated by the mind itself. Hence, the mediated mind content must come from the subject's short-term or long-term memory since it must have some permanence to be auto-mediated. This essay is not primarily about memories of conscious experience. Instead, it is about consciousness, which is argued to be ontologically identical to immediate mind content, otherwise known as phenomenal experience.

It is argued that analytic philosophy's toolbox, which contains replicable experiment and formal mathematical and

deductive logic, is inadequate to study consciousness. Instead, a rational inquiry into the nature of consciousness leads to nondualistic insight, which, in turn, justifies the use of inductive reason to study consciousness. Hence, the investigation method consists of applying the principles of rational thought. The principles of rational thought are the following:
1. The law of non-contradiction, indicating that, within the same context, two meaningful contradictory statements cannot both be true. Attributed to Aristotle.
2. The law of the excluded middle, stating that, within the same context, a meaningful statement cannot be both true and false. Also from Aristotle.
3. The law of identity of indiscernibles, also known as the law of identity, asserting that two substances sharing all properties are ontologically identical. Credited to Leibniz.
4. The principle of sufficient reason, also from Leibniz. It is, as Leibniz writes in the Monadologie (1714), the principle ". . . by virtue of which we consider that we can find no true or existing fact, no true assertion, without there being a sufficient reason why it is thus and not otherwise, although most of the time these reasons cannot be known to us."

Irrational theories and beliefs disregard at least one of these principles. The principles are conducive to meaningful, coherent, and natural explanations of phenomena and their greatest common denominator. A rational theory is meaningful, coherent, and corresponds to all relevant facts, including empirical facts insofar as available and attainable. With natural is meant that the explanations are not unnatural or supernatural: While they may be counterintuitive, their implications don't contradict the a priori causal and contiguous way the human mind may understand the world based on the singularly present way it experiences that world. In other words, they avoid the contradiction of claiming an

## 1. SCOPE AND METHOD

understanding of what is unintelligible.

# 2

# IRRATIONAL WESTERN CONSCIOUSNESS THEORIES

The interaction problem, in this essay broadly referring to the two-way causal interaction between consciousness and "the rest of the world," or "not consciousness," renders all dualistic consciousness theories irrational because they imply an ontic separation of cause and effect. Such a discontinuous process between the dually split world elements contradicts the singularly present way the human mind experiences the world, hence, is supernatural and unintelligible.

All consciousness theories that involve conceiving something that is not consciousness must be considered dualisms to avoid a contradiction. Monisms conceive consciousness in several ways, e.g., as entirely mental, physical, or a third substance. Monisms define what consciousness is, thereby implicitly defining the negation of consciousness: what consciousness is not. Hence, all monisms are implicitly dualistic: They require the conjecture that consciousness can know what consciousness is not, thereby making an implicit assumption of extrasensory perception by consciousness of something that is not consciousness. The crucial difference between monism and nondualism is that the latter considers that consciousness and the rest of the world, subject and object, are united but not conceivable, as will be clarified going forward.

Panpsychism promises a nondualistic account of consciousness, yet its analytic, bottom-up approach leads to conceiving consciousness as either an attribute of reality or an essence of a conceivable reality. In both cases, panpsychism reveals itself as an implicit dualism because it asserts conceptual knowledge of consciousness: what it is and is not. Hence, all types of panpsychism, including micropsychism, cosmopsychism, and panprotopsychism, are irrational because they entail the interaction problem between consciousness and not consciousness.

Leibniz's monads theory, an 18th-century panpsychism in which many irreducible mental substances make up the world, is also dualistic, hence not rational, since it involves an unresolved interaction problem between the monads and mental processes.

Physicalism, insofar as it is physical monism, solves the interaction problem by denying the existence of consciousness. However, the present immediacy of consciousness makes consciousness undeniable because the present leaves the subject no time to deny it. A subject needs to be conscious to claim not to have consciousness. Hence, consciousness is real.

This argument for the existence of consciousness is similar to the Cartesian "I think, therefore I am." In the Meditations (1641), Descartes defines thought as "what happens in me such that I am immediately conscious of it, insofar as I am conscious of it." So, his thought is the conscious experience rather than merely cognition. He uses the observation of his inability to doubt that he doubts to claim certainty of the knowledge of being a thinking entity—that, therefore, must exist.

Pantheism is potentially rational, depending on the definition of God—or, technically, the lack of such a definition. If God is interpreted as the inconceivable subject-object concurrence that is consciousness, pantheism equals nondualism, thereby avoiding the interaction problem. In that case, God is ontologically identical to the Tao of Eastern metaphysics, which is also ontologically identical to the nonduality, as will be discussed. However, if God is considered partly or entirely separate from consciousness, pantheism is a dualism and not rational.

Panentheism, which considers the universe a part of God, is not rational because it is a transcendent knowledge claim: God is bigger than the universe. Transcendent knowledge claims are irrational because they constitute a contradiction in terms: knowledge of the unknowable.

The next subchapter explains why Western philosophy currently prefers the analytic approach to consciousness and why this approach fails to provide a rational account of consciousness.

# 3

# THE LIMITATIONS OF ANALYTIC PHILOSOPHY

A historic cornerstone of analytic philosophy is one of the most influential works in Western modern philosophy: Hume's "An Enquiry Concerning Human Understanding" (1748). A fundamental principle of Humean skepticism and its heir, Popper's scientific skepticism, is that reason is to be distrusted because it is subjective. The implicit assumption of analytic philosophy is that empirical matters of fact and logical deductions thereof are instead imbued with some mind-independent truth, a certain degree of objectivity.

Philosophers in the analytic tradition are thought leaders in the West. In line with neuroscience, their analytic tradition leads them to approach consciousness matters with empiricism and deductive logic. Analysis is an investigation of the components of the whole and their relations, so it conceives knowledge bottom-up in parts and always involves implicit or explicit dualism. Their dualism renders analytic consciousness theories irrational. Whenever the conscious mind tries to find mind-independent knowledge by analyzing itself, it fails because it cannot detach from itself. A bottom-up analysis of the conscious mind in the hope of finding mind-independent knowledge about it is the mental equivalent of chasing one's tail or lifting oneself by the bootstraps.

The only rational approach to understanding consciousness starts top-down, integrally, before analysis. An analogy may clarify what I mean: If one were asked to see one's vision, how would one go about it? List the things one sees and analyze them? Analyze a retina under a microscope? None of these are necessary: One accomplishes the task simply by seeing. Likewise, if one is to know consciousness, how does one go about it? Categorize the phenomena in consciousness and analyze them? Anatomic study of the brain? Although exceedingly interesting, none of these are necessary. As we see vision simply by seeing, so do we know consciousness simply by knowing. All subjects know their consciousness entirely because one cannot distance oneself from one's consciousness.

Even so, analysis helps understand consciousness. Yet, all relevant facts should be considered to arrive at rational conclusions concerning consciousness. A bottom-up analysis of consciousness misses the pre-conceptual big picture of subjectivity. In contrast, this essay aims for the top-down comprehension of consciousness's highest common denominator by considering all relevant facts. Consciousness is understood when nondualism is understood, and nondualism is understood when the nonduality (the subject-object concurrence) is understood. The starting point for understanding consciousness this way is the fact that all subjects have complete knowledge of it, albeit from a first-person perspective.

One cannot not know one's consciousness because it equals one's existence. The manifestation of the self, the body, and the rest of the objectified, conceived world is contingent on consciousness. For example, as Descartes concluded in the Meditations based on the phantom pain phenomenon, the location of the body is the product of the mind's imagination. Likewise, it is not the brain that causes the conscious mind but

## 3. THE LIMITATIONS OF ANALYTIC PHILOSOPHY

the conscious mind that imagines the brain, notwithstanding the factual correlations between brain areas and the conscious experience. The crucial point is that such and other facts cannot be known to constitute an objective, mind-independent reality because humans lack the extrasensory perception required for gathering knowledge beyond consciousness.

Hume's skepticism, particularly his problem of induction, invalidates the preceding rational induction of consciousness knowledge. So, before I continue my argument in favor of nondualism, it is incumbent upon me to refute his skepticism. Hume demonstrates that we cannot have certain knowledge about the world as our knowledge of it transpires either as matters of fact or as relations of ideas. Matters of fact don't provide certainty about the world because of the problem of induction, and relations of ideas are based on a priori knowledge that is the product of custom and habit, so they don't provide certainty about the world either. Yet, Hume's knowledge template comprises neither the Cartesian certainty of existing nor the fact that we can have any knowledge at all. Many, including Kant, have looked for the missing element in Hume's knowledge model but have failed to find it.

Nondualism gives solace: Hume's epistemological model only considers conceived knowledge and fails to acknowledge and include unconceived knowledge. The human conscious mind consists entirely of immediate and auto-mediated content: consciousness and memories of consciousness, unconceived and conceived knowledge, ontic and epistemic knowledge, the impermanent and the permanent, change and difference, the present and the not-present, real existence and what is unreal. The distinction between all these pairs of mind content, each of which, as will be demonstrated, consecutively identifies precisely the same pair of substances, is that the meaning of the former in the pair is entirely bound by present immediacy and the latter not. Immediate, unconceived knowledge equals consciousness and is indubitable because it equals the subject's existence, as per the Cartesian Cogito. Knowledge of consciousness cannot be denied without a contradiction. Unconceived knowledge, ontologically identical to consciousness, is necessarily true because it continuously empirically confirms itself. Thus, nondualism refutes Hume's skepticism.

# 4

# THE NON-EXISTENCE OF WHAT MEMORIES REFER TO

The law of identity of indiscernibles entails that immediate, unconceived knowledge is ontologically identical to both consciousness and the phenomenal experience because they share all properties: They refer to a substance that is singular (indivisible) in the present, immediate, private, and entirely known to the subject. Nondualism is based on the realization that only unconceived knowledge is real, which is why this substance can also be referred to as the nonduality.

In contrast, conceived knowledge refers to entities that cannot be known to exist beyond the mind's imagination. Numerous facts sustain this conclusion, for example:
1. The mind needs some time to conceive something, so whatever it conceives must be something in the past. The past cannot be known to exist anymore in the present.
2. The present's hallmark is continuous change and renewal: Nothing remains unchanged. Yet, whatever is conceived and in short-term or long-term memory is

necessarily something with a certain permanence—hence, it cannot be known to exist.
3. Determination is negation: Whatever is conceived has at least one opposite in its negation. Yet, the immediate, real present cannot be negated since it is durationless. Accordingly, the present is indivisible and lacks an opposite.

This rational metaphysical analysis leads to the counterintuitive, sweeping conclusions of nondualism:
1. Nothing that has ever been written or thought about can be known to exist. What thoughts, concepts, numbers, equations, laws of physics, and words refer to is necessarily something with permanence—otherwise, we wouldn't be able to remember them.
2. Only consciousness is real, and it is entirely impermanent and private. Once one communicates about one's consciousness or its aspects, one must conceptualize it. The meaning of what is conceptualized is no longer bound by present immediacy.
3. Change is real, and permanence is imagined.
4. Consciousness, the present, and change are ontologically indiscernible because they share all properties. All three are mutually required to manifest themselves and always appear in perfect unison.
5. Existence is the undeniable, durationless, inconceivable singularity of present change.
6. Conceived change, which constitutes difference (contrast), isn't real because one can only conceive knowledge by imagining permanence. In other words, differences don't exist.
7. Multiplicity is imagined. Otherwise stated, conceiving the existence of separate substances is irrational.

Nondualism implies that none of the following concepts can be known to refer to anything real: The self, all other people and creatures, objects, spacetime, detached causes and effects, quantum and other submicroscopic objects, laws of physics, equations, definitions, and words. Conversely, the following immediate, spontaneous conscious experiences must be considered real: free will (agency), sensory experience, and feelings, including positive and negative feelings and feelings of truthfulness. The latter does not imply that subjectivity automatically leads to truthful knowledge. Rather, reason leads to rational beliefs that may increase our confidence in the trustworthiness of truthfulness feelings.

An argument against nondualism is that the world's perceived continuity requires a mind-independent world: When I sit down on a chair, it is usually, fortunately, still in the same place I found before I decided to sit down. We can forecast, for example, tomorrow's weather because it seems that the mind-independent world soldiers on when our minds go to sleep at night. The argument that defuses the continuity argument against nondualism is that nondualism implies that consciousness is not merely a subject, separate from the objective reality, but subject and object at once. Hence, there is certainly value in predicting the world and conceiving facts about it. However, it must be understood that these facts do not reveal reality since they are mind-dependent.

Another argument against nondualism is the paradox that consciousness must be all-encompassing, while individuals have separate, different, and private conscious experiences referring to what seems to be the same world, albeit from different perspectives. This paradox is resolved by noticing that individual unconceived conscious experiences only become separate from those of other subjects after their conceptualization. Before conceptualization, they are limitless, without properties, all-encompassing, and shared because they are ontologically indiscernible.

## 5

# THE VIRTUOUS NONDUALISM AND REASON CIRCLE—AND ITS LIMITATIONS

The nondualistic realization of the inaccessibility of a mind-independent reality and truth implies that reason deserves to be the supreme scientific principle. The a priori principles of rational thought rest on the pervasive empirical fact of singularly present conscious experience, which entails temporal and spatial contiguity since cause and effect must be unified in the unconceived present conscious experience, only to be separated in the imagination of a conceiving mind. The validity of mathematical axioms and empirical verification's critical role in science rests on the same intrinsically empirical a priori facts as those that sustain inducing knowledge about consciousness using the principles of rational thought. In nondualism, there is no contradiction between reason and empiricism because all knowledge must come from consciousness—hence, be empirical. Thus, nondualism leads to reason, and reason leads to nondualism, and both sustain applying the principles of rational thought to study consciousness.

Nondual awareness can only be gained in first-person

## 5. THE VIRTUOUS NONDUALISM AND REASON CIRCLE—AND ITS LIMITATIONS

conscious experience since the nonduality that is consciousness is known privately. A subject is a first-person consciousness, and when one conceives oneself or others as separate subjects, one merely has conceived projections of consciousness for which there are no rational grounds to assume that they exist beyond imagination.

By applying the principles of rational thought, we can determine the limits of our potential knowledge and understanding of consciousness. Notably, we can infer that the efficient cause of consciousness is unknowable—as follows: Only subjects, first persons, know the consciousness phenomenon, which is strictly private on account of its present immediacy. To know the efficient cause of a phenomenon, one needs to know that phenomenon. It is not possible to understand something one doesn't know. An explanation consists of an explanandum, that which is to be explained, and an explanans, that which explains. So, all meaningful explanations contain the explanandum they refer to.

Only the subject has access to the explanandum that is consciousness, which is private. Hence, only the subjects themselves are candidates to determine the explanans (efficient cause) of "their" consciousness. The efficient cause must, by definition, be within consciousness for the subject to be aware of it. Consciousness is immediate, impermanent, and indivisible. In this constellation, no rational explanans is conceivable except for the explanans being the explanandum. Thus, consciousness's efficient cause can be either considered itself or unknowable. In this way, consciousness is ultimate, ontic knowledge. Consciousness, phenomenally entirely known, must remain conceptually unexplained beyond conceiving it as its own efficient cause. No explanation can account for the consciousness phenomenon because consciousness is strictly non-conceptual.

Despite the rational conclusion that consciousness is conceptually inexplicable, nondualism is not a "mysterianism" because the fully known unconceived knowledge that is consciousness is necessarily true, as demonstrated previously.

We can now answer whether consciousness is fundamental: Yes, it is because it is ultimate, ontic knowledge, and nothing but consciousness can be known to be real. However, consciousness cannot be known to be a fundamental building block of reality because the rational position toward reality is agnostic since it is demonstrably unknowable.

In summary, nondualism's account of consciousness is unique in not requiring supernatural assumptions while agreeing with the ubiquitous empirical fact of singularly present conscious experience. Nondualism involves the following:

1. Consciousness is indubitable and entirely known to subjects but only in its unconceived, private state.
2. Only consciousness can be known to be real.
3. Consciousness lacks a knowable efficient cause. Hence, it is ontic knowledge.
4. Consciousness is the uncountable, indivisible, limitless concurrence of subject and object. The existence of an objective world in which separate objects and subjects exist is an illusion. Ontic multiplicity can only be known to exist in the conscious imagination. Hence, consciousness is inconceivable because conceived knowledge necessarily refers to separate entities, if only in contrast to the conceived entities as their negation.
5. Rational knowledge must be mind-dependent. Mind-independent knowledge, which includes all conjecture of detached causes and effects, is either fiction or faith, and science should refrain from making claims about it.
6. Unlike consciousness itself, memories of consciousness are marked by their potential negation. Such memories constitute epistemic knowledge that refers to non-existing entities. Even so, epistemic knowledge can be factual, rational, and highly relevant.
7. The substance consciousness is ontologically identical to change and to the present.

# 6

# THE INCONCEIVABLE NATURE OF CONSCIOUSNESS

How can one fathom the nature of singular, limitless consciousness without conceiving it? For millennia, spiritual teachers have taught meditation techniques to do so. However, the rational mind has every opportunity to do so as well. Rational beliefs about consciousness help to fathom it. Understanding consciousness in its non-conceptual, real form is less impeded by its complexity than by mental resistance to the perceived void left by the inexistence of all conceived entities, including the entire material world, all people and other creatures, and the past and future. The human mind's evolutionary birthright lies in conceiving differences (contrasts): biological threats and catalysts. Hence, the mind has difficulty recognizing that differences, while vital to the organism sustaining consciousness, don't exist beyond its imagination.

Nondualism is not an a-realism but a reality agnosticism. Reality—which must be an objective world separate from subjects if we rationally insist on excluding the meaningless middle—is a faith-based notion because it cannot be known to exist without resorting to supernatural assumptions about a magical connection between the mind world and the mind-independent world. Facts cannot reveal reality, even when they are as brilliant and truthful as mathematical logic and the empirically confirmed laws of physics. Reality is not unlike a transcendental god: religiously revered yet demonstrably unknowable.

However, the inconceivable, real, immediately present conscious experience is entirely known to subjects. It is inextricably intertwined with the physical world and the universe, including cause and effect, past and future, and all creatures in it—all of which cannot be conceived without breaching their ontic concurrence. Everything is consciousness because there is no sufficient reason to assume that consciousness and the past, present, and future world have separate existences. Hence, consciousness is limitless and inconceivable because what concepts refer to is, by definition, determined and bounded. This nonduality that is consciousness lacks a knowable efficient cause and is ontologically identical to change and to the present, both of which are also intrinsically inconceivable. In other words, conceiving is real, but what it conceives is not. Knowing is real, but what it knows is not. Experience is real, but what it experiences is not. Change is real, but what changes (difference) is not. Being is real, but what exists is not. Existence is fundamentally what existence is like.

Consciousness is entirely known in its unconceived state yet is inconceivable due to its impermanence and lack of a knowable efficient cause. This agrees with the first two lines of Lao Tzu's Tao Te Ching (6th century BCE): The Tao that can be told - is not the true Tao. Ontologically, Lao Tzu's Tao identifies the same substance as consciousness.

# 7
# NONDUALISTIC EPISTEMOLOGY

The nondualistic paradigm, based on the realization that we don't have access to anything that is not consciousness, entails that all concepts (conceived, epistemic knowledge) can be defined as memories of experience—experience by the subject itself or communicated by other subjects. Insofar as memories are not unconsciously acquired—inborn or subliminally gained—they must be conceived from real or imagined experience. The evolutionary purpose of concepts is to represent imagined experience for motivation and cognition.

Both ontic and epistemic knowledge, insofar as within a subject's awareness, are presently immediately experienced. However, epistemic knowledge results from the intentionality of real, presently immediate mental states (thoughts, hopes, desires, intuitions, etc.) that refer to concepts. In other words, epistemic knowledge is the real experience of imagined experience.

Nondualistic epistemology does not make a distinction between "subjective" qualitative and "objective" quantitative (mathematical, logical) knowledge since all epistemic knowledge must reflect the all-encompassing subject-object concurrence that is consciousness. As "blue" represents an imaginary experience of seeing a color, so does, e.g., the concept "three days" represent an imaginary experience—akin to counting three sunrises.

Although epistemic knowledge can be public and shared, its meaning is always privately experienced. Without private subjective experience, the concepts "blue" and "three days" are meaningless. We cannot verify if what "blue" and "three days" are like in the immediate conscious experience of any two subjects is the same, even though we seem to have remarkably similar experiences.

In contrast to epistemic knowledge (imagined experience), ontic knowledge (real experience, consciousness) has no intentionality and can be thought of as referring to nothing or to itself. Although consciousness is private from a first-person viewpoint, there is no individuality in the subject-object concurrence. Hence, the distinction between public and private knowledge is meaningless at the ontic level. This resolves the paradox that consciousness is epistemically private but ontically shared.

The privateness of imagined experience entails that interaction between subjects can only occur at the ontic level of real experience (unconceived consciousness, the present, change). In other words, epistemic knowledge (imaginary experience) cannot be an immediate efficient cause in the world unless it translates into real experience, e.g., agency experience.

The defining trait of rational knowledge, as opposed to fiction and faith-based knowledge, is that the imaginary experience it represents is a faithful reflection of real experience. How can we tell if this is the case? One person's imagination can be convincing to many. Since there is no mind-independent truth, the answer is ultimately subjective. Yet, the principles of rational thought, which, in nondualism, are compatible with the scientific method because the world is ontologically identical with consciousness, have stood the test of time as the epistemological rationality reference because they are based on a priori knowledge of pervasive singularly present experience. They have been challenged by Hume and, more recently, by Copenhagen quantum mechanics interpretation proponents, but, as I will now argue based on nondualistic insight, unreasonably so.

To summarize my previously mentioned epistemological argument against Humean skepticism: Since consciousness is ontic, it is neither deducible nor empirically verifiable. Hence, inductive reason based on the rules of rational thought is a valid means of studying consciousness.

My argument against the Copenhagen interpretation of quantum mechanics (hereafter referred to as Copenhagen) is that it is a dualistic theory that involves the interaction problem. A central implication of Copenhagen is that the measurement of a quantum object property immediately and discontinuously changes the ontic status of an entangled object in another location at wave function collapse. This hypothesized causal discontinuity is why Copenhagen proponents may doubt the principles of rational thought.

Copenhagen implies that not the local mechanical measurement process but the mental realization of the epistemic measurement knowledge is the efficient cause of such an ontic status change. Here, Copenhagen is dualistic because it assumes that the causing subject is ontically divorced from the affected object. It maintains that the immaterial mind is separate from the physical world it affects through what must be telekinesis—an implicitly supernatural hypothesis to solve the interaction problem.

Copenhagen mistakenly considers that measurements conceive reality. Copenhagen fails to incorporate the rational inference that the mind has no access to mind-independent knowledge: Epistemic knowledge is imagined experience only and cannot be an immediate efficient cause in the world.

Copenhagen's ontic, discrete interpretation of measurement effects and quantum jumps has been empirically falsified by experiments described in several publications.

"Paradox in Wave-Particle Duality"[1] falsifies Copenhagen's implication that quantum objects don't exhibit wave-like properties after determining their locations. "To catch and reverse a quantum jump mid-flight"[2] falsifies Copenhagen's hypothesis that quantum jumps are fundamentally discrete events. Bohmian mechanics is a counterexample of a quantum mechanics interpretation that does not require Copenhagen's causal discontinuity, as described in "A Suggested Interpretation of the Quantum Theory in Terms of Hidden Variables, I and II."[3] Hence, Copenhagen is not a rational theory and is to be rejected as an argument against the validity of the principles of rational thought.

---

[1] Afshar, S.S., Flores, E., McDonald, K.F. *et al.* Paradox in Wave-Particle Duality. *Found Phys* **37**, 295–305 (2007). https://doi.org/10.1007/s10701-006-9102-8.
[2] Minev, Z., Mundhada, S., Shankar, S. *et al.* To catch and reverse a quantum jump mid-flight. *Nature* **570**, 200–204 (2019). https://doi.org/10.1038/s41586-019-1287-z.
[3] Bohm, D.: 1952, A Suggested Interpretation of the Quantum Theory in Terms of Hidden Variables, I and II. *Physical Review* **85**, 166–179, 180–193. https://doi.org/10.1103/PhysRev.85.180.

# 8

# DISCUSSION

A potential objection to nondualism is that the symbiotic relationship between inductive reason and nondualism is based on a circular argument. However, nonduality implies that all consciousness theories share this predicament: Knowledge of consciousness, hence of the world, is necessarily self-reflective. Yet, unlike other consciousness theories, nondualism agrees with the pervasive empirical fact of singularly present conscious experience and the a priori knowledge derived from it.

Another objection to nondualism may result from being too dissimilar from the prevailing analytic approach to consciousness. The analytic paradigm may make inductive reason seem less rational than deductive reason, and the claim that analytic consciousness theories are irrational seem outrageous. This may be a roadblock to the consideration of nondualism. It may be dismissed either as a mysterianism or as unscientific because it goes beyond skepticism in Hume's and Popper's tradition, even though it demonstrates the availability of indubitable knowledge and empirical facts that support its conclusions. Nondualism may also be dismissed as a form of neutral monism, which it is not because neutral monism conceives consciousness as neither mental nor physical. In contrast, nondualism acknowledges on rational grounds that the human mind cannot conceive what the substance consciousness is—or not—beyond its identification through its properties as an inconceivable, ontologically indivisible substance.

There is supporting evidence for nondualism in physics: In his "Time and Classical and Quantum Mechanics: Indeterminacy vs Discontinuity," Lynds postulates there is not a precise static instant in time underlying a dynamical physical process at which the relative position of a body in relative motion or a specific physical magnitude would theoretically be precisely determined. He concludes it is exactly because of this that time (relative interval as indicated by a clock) and the continuity of a physical process are possible, with there being a necessary trade-off of all precisely determined physical values at a time, for their continuity through time.[4] The inexistence of spacetime as a precisely determinable physical magnitude thus deduced from the continuity of physical processes supports nondualism because nondualism entails that the universe is change only.

The shared ontological identity of consciousness and the present that marks nondualism is also coherent with physics' observer-dependent relativity of simultaneity and spacetime. In contrast, dualism's implicitly or explicitly presumed ontic split between observers and what they observe is not supported by special and general relativity.

Conversely, physics may benefit from nondualism because the impossibility of mind-independent knowledge it entails has implications for quantum mechanics interpretations. Specifically, it offers a more nuanced understanding of the wavefunction collapse phenomenon, as postulated in the

---

[4] Lynds, P. Time and Classical and Quantum Mechanics: Indeterminacy Versus Discontinuity. *Found Phys Lett* **16**, 343–355 (2003). https://doi.org/10.1023/A:1025361725408.

## 8. DISCUSSION

Copenhagen interpretation of quantum mechanics, during the measurement of a quantum superposition.

Particularly, since nondualism rejects any discontinuous emergence of reality through measurement, the determination of a quantum object's observable cannot be understood as forcing a superposition of quantum states into a definite eigenstate. Additionally, in a nondual interpretation of quantum mechanics, a measured eigenstate is not considered to possess mind-independent existence. In other words, quantum objects and their properties cannot be known to exist either before or after measurement beyond their conceptualization.

# CONCLUSION

All monisms are implicit dualisms of consciousness versus not consciousness because they assume that consciousness is conceivable. Implicit and explicit dualisms are not rational because they involve the interaction problem between consciousness and what is not consciousness. In contrast, nondualism is predicated on the inconceivability of consciousness and the rational fact that the universe must be consciousness only because nothing else can be known to be real. Moreover, consciousness lacks a knowable efficient cause because it is inconceivable, private, and impermanent—despite being undeniable. For these reasons, consciousness is fundamental, and our universe is essentially what it is like to us.

Reason demands that the word reality means something existing beyond ever-changing consciousness, as it implies persistent substance. Reality is a faith-based notion because it is unknowable. Hence, consciousness cannot be known to be a fundamental attribute of reality because reason forbids reality knowledge claims. Reason calls on science to relegate the mind-independent world to fiction and faith.

# ACKNOWLEDGMENT

I wish to thank Ioana Andreea Stoian, M.D., for providing invaluable feedback.

# ABOUT THE AUTHOR

What is a "zengineer"? A word you won't find in the dictionary! It's a bridge builder between Zen and reason. Meet Marcel Eschauzier, a Dutch native living in Belgium with his better half. He spent years traveling, doing corporate gigs and living across cultures. A nondual awakening in 2016 made him trade his suitcases for an inner journey and a desire to share the sublime simplicity he found. Five years later, his books were regularly topping Amazon's philosophy charts. A practical engineer at heart, Marcel is also passionate about nonduality's meaning for physics—hard to overstate but typically overlooked. Other interests include long walks and losing staring contests to the dog. Marcel holds a Master of Science in Industrial Engineering and Management Science from the Eindhoven University of Technology.

❈

*Dear reader,*

Thank you for reading. If you feel like it, please leave a five-star rating on your platform of choice or tell a friend. Indie authors like me really don't stand a chance without your support. ♥
amazon.com/review/create-review?&asin=B0CLCXNC46
goodreads.com/book/show/200213548
I also welcome your suggestions and thoughts. Below are some ways to get in touch with me.
Undividedly,

*Marcel*

simplynondual.com
nondual.gumroad.com (Marcel's Booktique)
simplynondual.substack.com
x.com/simplynondual
facebook.com/simplynondual
linkedin.com/in/marceleschauzier
youtube.com/@simplynondual
books2read.com/marceleschauzier

Made in the USA
Coppell, TX
02 June 2025